MICHAEL ♔ JACKSON
FOR UKULELE

Cover Photo: Time & Life Pictures / Getty Images Contributor

ISBN 978-1-4803-8770-6

HAL•LEONARD® CORPORATION
7777 W. BLUEMOUND RD. P.O. BOX 13819 MILWAUKEE, WI 53213

Visit Hal Leonard Online at
www.halleonard.com

Bad

Words and Music by Michael Jackson

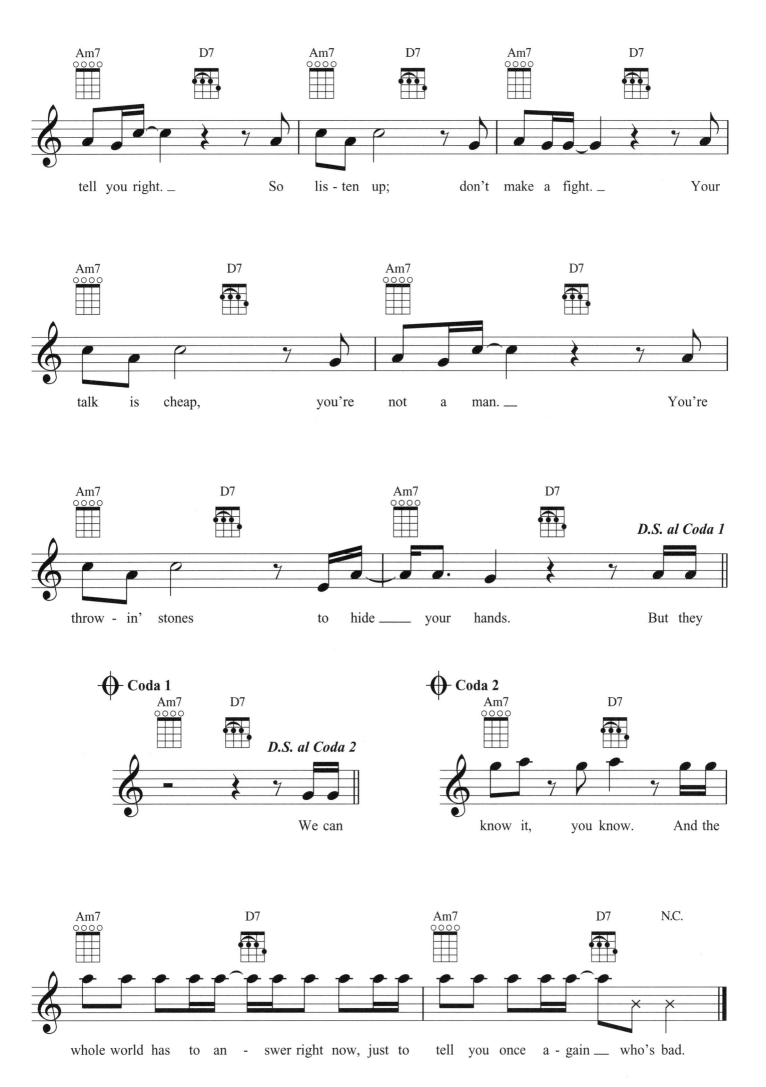

tell you right. _ So lis-ten up; don't make a fight. _ Your

talk is cheap, you're not a man. __ You're

throw-in' stones to hide ___ your hands. But they

Coda 1

D.S. al Coda 2

We can

Coda 2

know it, you know. And the

whole world has to an-swer right now, just to tell you once a-gain _ who's bad.

Beat It

Words and Music by Michael Jackson

First note

Verse
Moderately fast

1. They told him, "Don't you ev - er come a - round here. Don't
2.–4. *See additional lyrics*

wan - na see your face; you bet - ter dis - ap - pear." The

fi - re's in their eyes and their words are real - ly clear. So

1., 3.
beat it, just beat it.

2., 4.
beat it. But you

Additional Lyrics

2. You better run, you better do what you can.
   Don't wanna see no blood; don't be a macho man.
   You wanna be tough; better do what you can.
   So beat it. But you wanna be bad.

3. They're out to get you; better leave while you can.
   Don't wanna be a boy; you wanna be a man.
   You wanna stay alive; better do what you can.
   So beat it, just beat it.

4. You have to show them that you're really not scared.
   You're playin' with your life; this ain't no truth or dare.
   They'll kick you, then they'll beat you, then they'll tell you it's fair.
   So beat it. But you wanna be bad.

Ben

Words by Don Black
Music by Walter Scharf

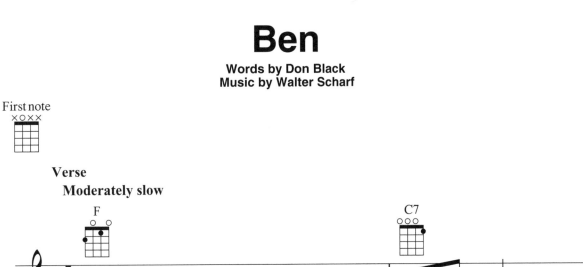

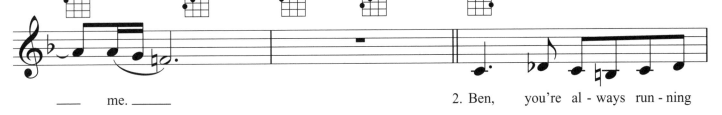

here and there; you feel you're not want-ed an - y - where.

If you ev - er look be - hind and don't like what you

find, there's some - thing you should know: you've got a place to ___

Bridge

___ go. ___ I used to say

I and me; now it's us, now it's we. I

used to say I and me; now it's us,

Outro-Verse

now it's we.   Ben,   most peo - ple would turn

you a - way;   I   don't lis - ten to a

word they say.   They   don't see you as I

do;   I wish they would try to.   I'm sure they'd think a -

gain if they had a friend like Ben,   (like Ben,)   like ___

rit.

Ben, _____ (like Ben,)   like   Ben. _____

Billie Jean

Words and Music by Michael Jackson

1. She was more like a beau - ty queen from a mov - ie scene.
2. *See additional lyrics*

I said don't mind, but what do ____ you mean I ____ am the one ____

____ who will dance on the floor in the round?

She said I ____ am the one ____ who will dance

on the floor in the round.

She told me her name was Bil - lie Jean as she caused a scene.

Then ev - 'ry head turned with eyes ___ that dreamed of be - ing the one ___

___ who will dance on the floor in the round.

Pre-Chorus

(1.) Peo - ple al - ways told ___ me, be
(2.) *See additional lyrics*

care - ful of what you do. Don't go a - round ___ break - in' young girls' hearts. ___

And Moth - er al - ways told ___ me: Be

care - ful of who you love. Be care - ful of what you do, ___ 'cause the

Chorus

lie be - comes _ the truth. Hey. _____ Bil - lie Jean ___ is

not my lov - er. She's just a girl ___ who

claims that I ___ am the one, _____ but the

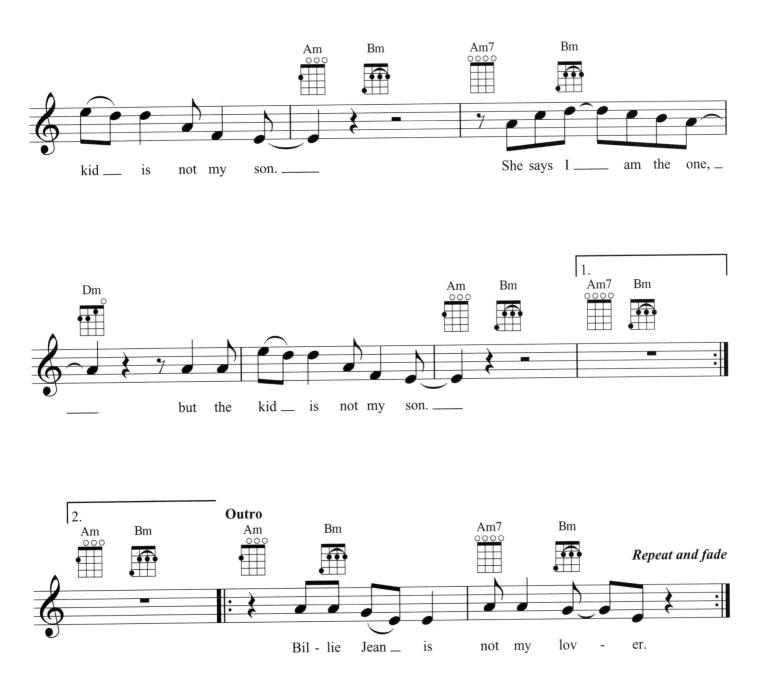

kid __ is not my son. _____ She says I _____ am the one, _

_____ but the kid __ is not my son. _____

Outro

Repeat and fade

Bil - lie Jean __ is not my lov - er.

Additional Lyrics

2. For forty days and for forty nights, law was on her side.
But who can stand when she's in demand, her schemes and plans,
'Cause we danced on the floor in the round?
So take my strong advice: Just remember to always think twice.
She told my baby we'd danced till three,
And she looked at me, then showed a photo.
My baby cried; his eyes were like mine,
'Cause we danced on the floor in the round.

Pre-Chorus: People always told me: Be careful of what you do.
Don't go around breakin' young girls' hearts.
But you came and stood right by me, just a smell of sweet perfume.
This happened much too soon; she called me to her room. Hey.

Black or White

Words and Music by Michael Jackson

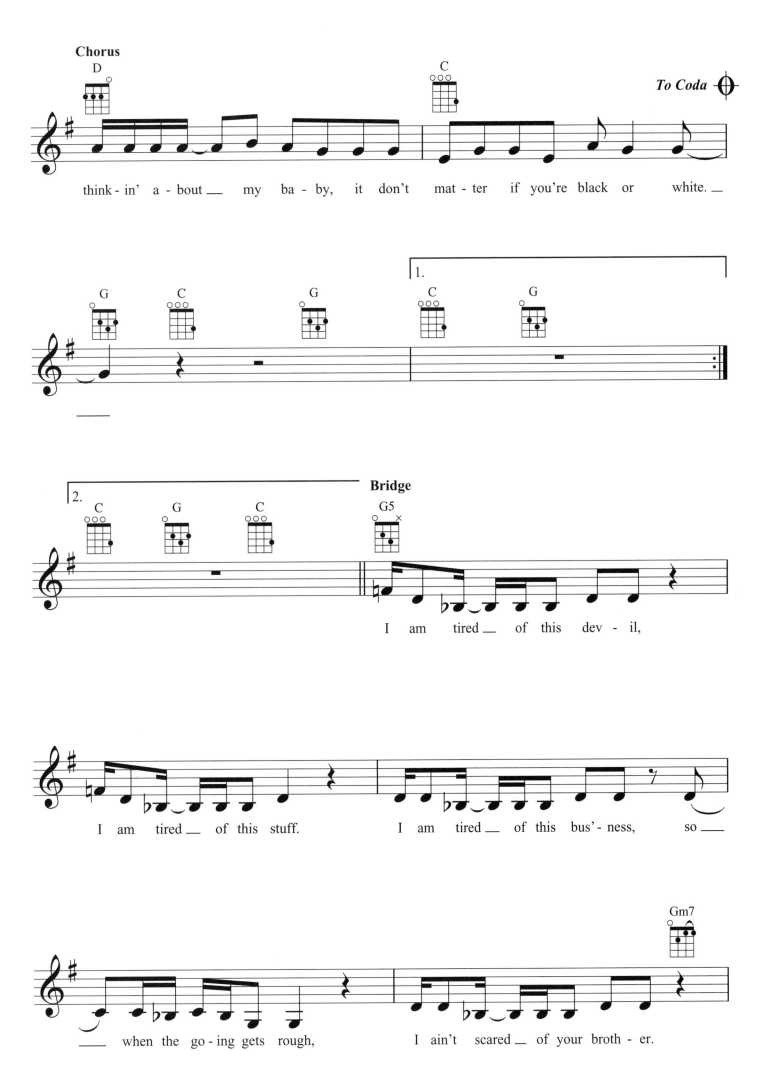

I ain't scared _ of no sheets.   I ain't scared _ of no - bod - y, girl, _

D.S. al Coda

_ when the go - in' gets mean.   Don't

Coda

Outro-Chorus

I _ said, if you're think - in' of be - ing my { ba - by, } it don't
                                              { broth - er, }

mat - ter if you're black or white. _

1.

I _ said, if you're

2.

Heal the World

Written and Composed by Michael Jackson

Dirty Diana

Written by Michael Jackson

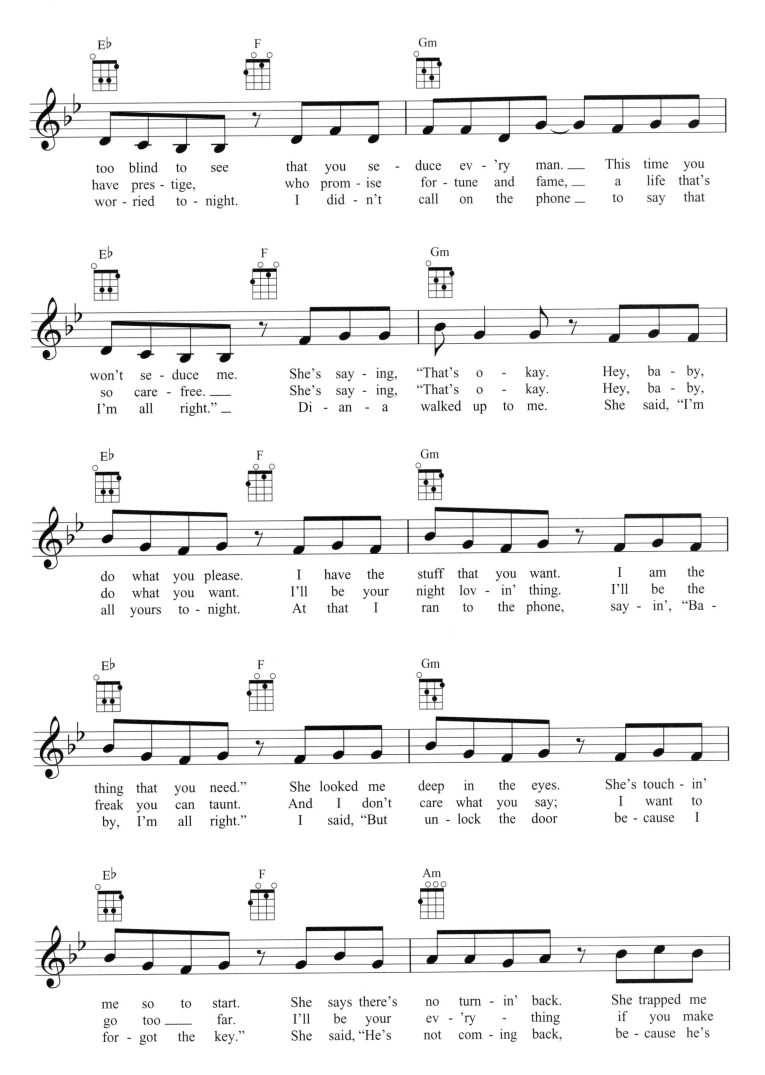

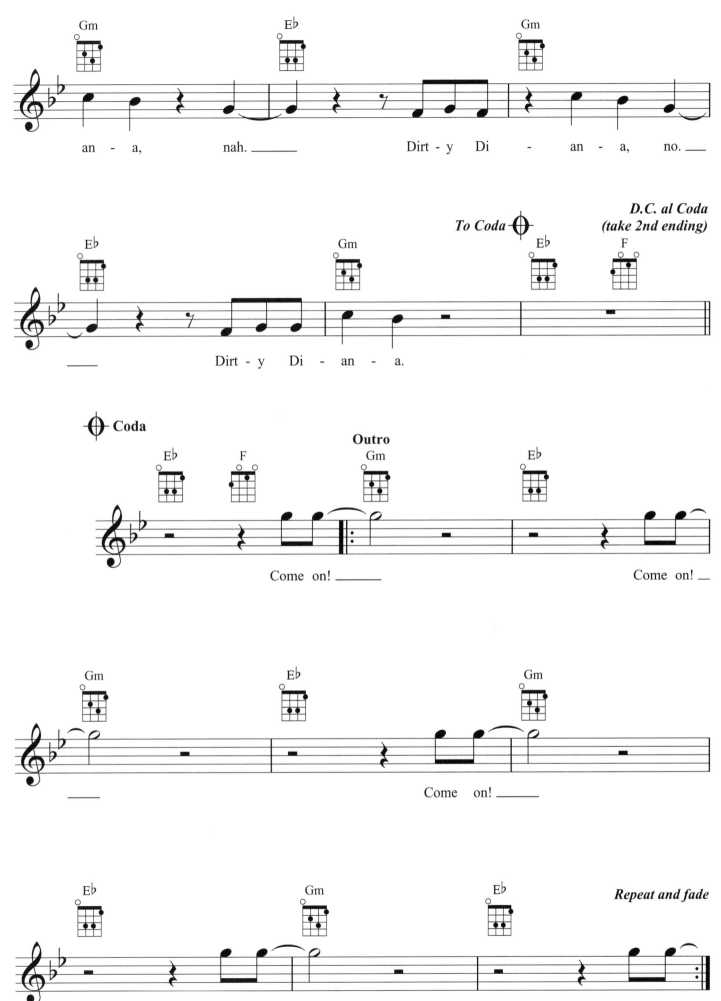

Don't Stop 'Til You Get Enough

Written by Michael Jackson

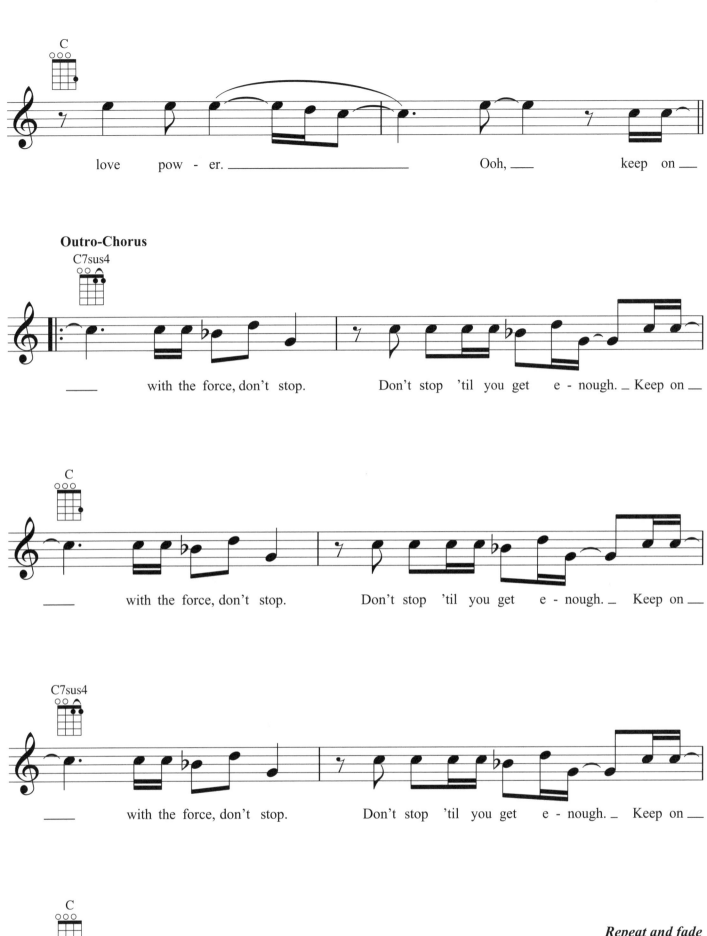

love pow - er. _____ Ooh, ___ keep on ___

Outro-Chorus

C7sus4

___ with the force, don't stop. Don't stop 'til you get e - nough. ___ Keep on ___

C

___ with the force, don't stop. Don't stop 'til you get e - nough. ___ Keep on ___

C7sus4

___ with the force, don't stop. Don't stop 'til you get e - nough. ___ Keep on ___

C

Repeat and fade

___ with the force, don't stop. Don't stop 'til you get e - nough. ___ Keep on ___

The Girl Is Mine

Words and Music by Michael Jackson

be - cause the dog - gone girl is mine.

To Coda

2. I don't

Bridge

I love you more than he. (Take you an - y - where.)

Well, I love you end - less - ly. (Lov - ing we will share.) So

come and go with me, two on the town.

But we both can - not have

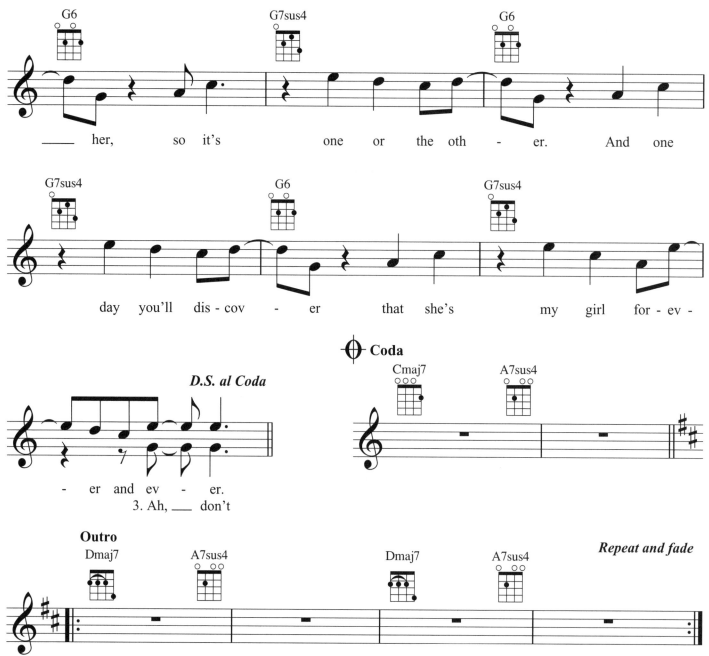

G6   G7sus4   G6

———— her,   so it's   one   or   the   oth -   er.   And   one

G7sus4   G6   G7sus4

day   you'll   dis - cov -   er   that   she's   my   girl   for - ev -

D.S. al Coda

⊕ **Coda**

Cmaj7   A7sus4

\- er   and   ev -   er.

3. Ah, —— don't

Outro

Dmaj7   A7sus4   Dmaj7   A7sus4

Repeat and fade

Lead vocal ad lib.

Additional Lyrics

2. I don't understand the way you think,
Saying that she's yours, not mine.
Sending roses and your silly dreams,
Really just a waste of time,
Because she's mine,
The doggone girl is mine.
Don't waste your time,
Because the doggone girl is mine.

3. Ah, don't build your hopes to be let down,
'Cause I really feel it's time.
I know she'll tell you I'm the one for her,
'Cause she said I blow her mind.
The girl is mine,
The doggone girl is mine.
Don't waste your time,
Because the doggone girl is mine.

Love Never Felt So Good

Words and Music by Michael Jackson and Paul Anka

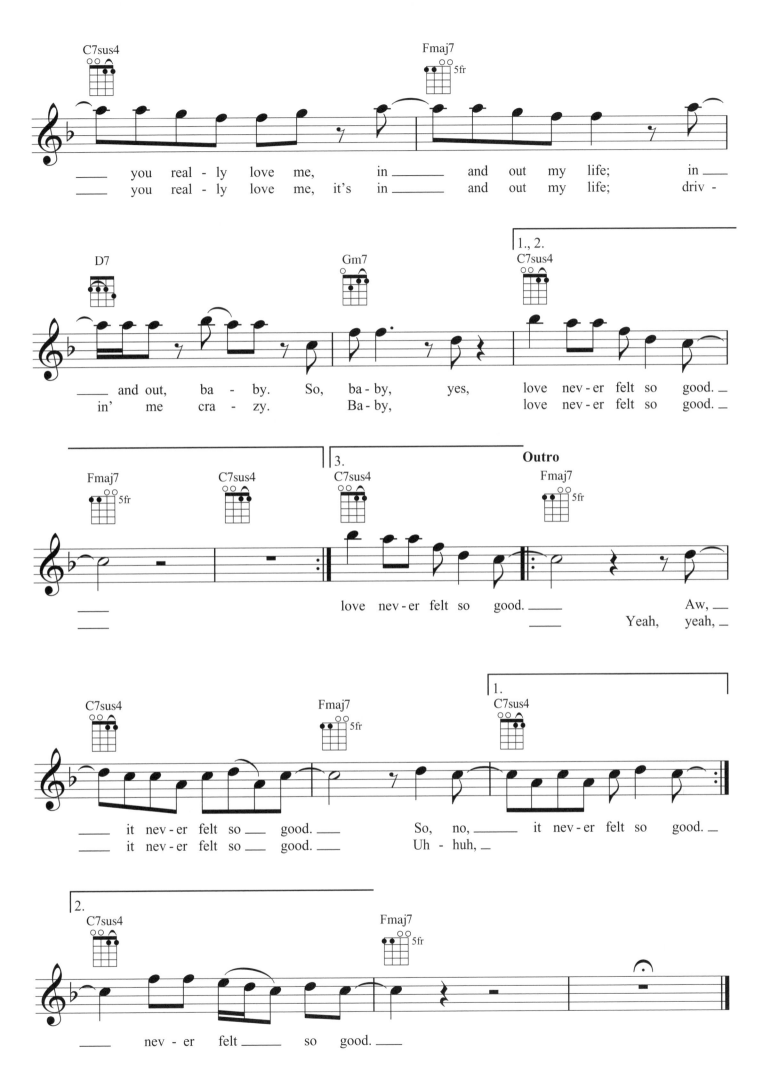

I Just Can't Stop Loving You

Written by Michael Jackson

E♭maj7   G7sus4

This time is for - ev - er; love is the an - swer.

Verse

C

Female: 2. I hear your voice ___ now; you are my choice ___ now,
(3.) night when the stars ___ shine, I pray in you I'll ___ find

Gm7   C

the love you bring. Heav-en's in my ___ heart; at
a love so true. *Female:* When morn-ing a - wakes ___ me, will

Gm7

your call I hear ___ harps, and an - gels sing. ___
you come and take ___ me? I'll wait for you. ___

Fmaj7

              3   *3*

_____ You know how I feel; this thing can't go wrong.
_____ *Male:* You know how I feel; I won't stop un - til

Fm   Am7

I can't live my life with - out you. ___
I hear your voice say - ing, "I do." *Female:* I do. *Male:* I
                                                        This

just can't hold on. *Female:* I feel _____ we be-long.
thing can't go wrong. *Male:* This feel - ing's so __ strong. *Female:* Well, __

Male: My life ain't worth liv - ing if I can't be with you.
my life ain't worth liv - ing *Both:* if I can't be with you.

Chorus

Both: I just can't stop lov - ing you. ____
I just can't stop lov - ing you. __

____ And if I stop, then tell me: just what __ will I do? __

1.

____ *Female:* 'Cause I just can't stop lov - ing you. ____ *Male:* 3. At

2.

_____ *Male:* I just can't stop lov - ing you. ____ *Female:* We can

Man in the Mirror

Words and Music by Glen Ballard and Siedah Garrett

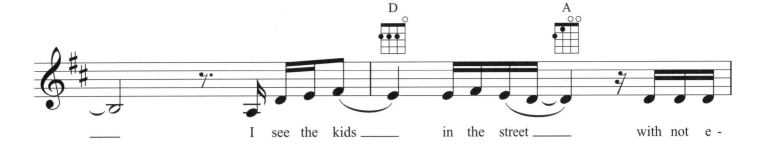

I see the kids _____ in the street _____ with not e-

nough to eat. Who am I to be blind, _ pre-tend-ing not to

see their _____ need? _____ A sum-mer's dis-re-gard,

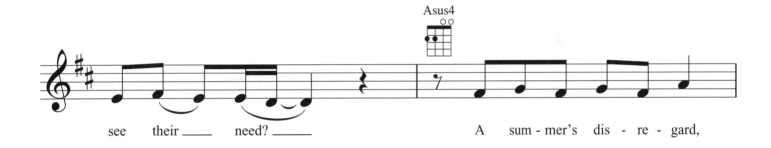

a bro-ken bot-tle top, and-a one _____ man's soul. _

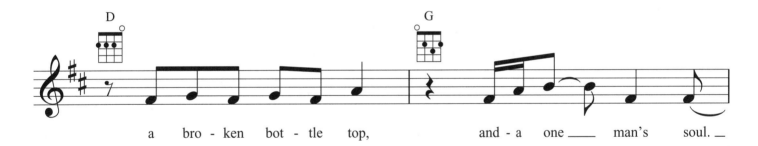

_____ They fol-low each oth-er on the wind,

you know, 'cause they got _____ no-where _ to go.

Additional Lyrics

2. I've been a victim of a selfish kind of love,
   It's time that I realize that there are some with no home, not a nickel to loan.
   Could it be really me, pretending that they're not alone?
   A widow deeply scarred, somebody's broken heart and a washed-out dream.
   They follow the pattern of the wind, you see,
   'Cause they got no place to be. That's why I'm starting with me.

Rock with You

Words and Music by Rod Temperton

Remember the Time

Words and Music by Michael Jackson, Teddy Riley and Bernard Belle

Pre-Chorus

51

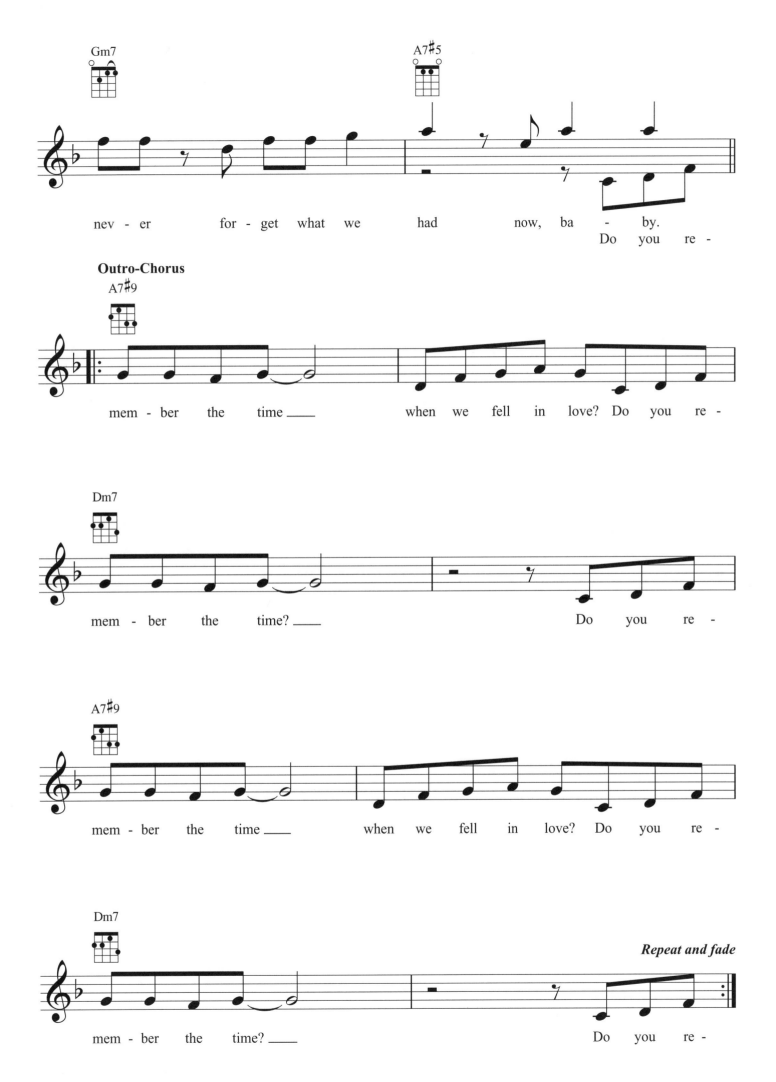

Outro-Chorus

Repeat and fade

Smooth Criminal

Words and Music by Michael Jackson

Thriller

Words and Music by Rod Temperton

it. You start to freeze as hor-ror looks you right be-tween the eyes. You're par-a-lyzed.

Chorus

'Cause this is thrill-er, thrill-er night, and no one's gon-na save you from the beast a-bout to strike. You know it's thrill-er, thrill-er night. You're fight-ing for your life in-side a

(See spoken text)

Additional Lyrics

2. You hear the door slam
   And realize there's nowhere left to run.
   You feel the cold hand
   And wonder if you'll ever see the sun.
   You close your eyes
   And hope that this is just imagination.
   But all the while,
   You hear the creature creepin' up behind.
   You're out of time, 'cause this is...

Chorus: Thriller, thriller night.
   There ain't no second chance
   Against the thing with forty eyes.
   Thriller, thriller night.
   You're fighting for your life inside a
   Killer thriller tonight.

3. They're out to get you.
   There's demons closin' in on every side.
   They will possess you
   Unless you change that number on your dial.
   Now is the time
   For you and I to cuddle close together.
   All through the night
   I'll save you from the terror on the screen.
   I'll make you see that this is...

Chorus: Thriller, thriller night.
   'Cause I can thrill you more
   Than any ghost would ever dare try.
   Thriller, thriller night.
   So let me hold you tight and share a
   Killer thriller tonight.

Spoken Text

Darkness falls across the land.
The midnight hour is close at hand.
Creatures crawl in search of blood
To terrorize y'all's neighborhood.
And whosoever shall be found
Without the soul for getting down
Must stand and face the hounds of hell
And rot inside a corpse's shell.

The foulest stench is in the air,
The funk of forty thousand years.
And grizzly ghouls from every tomb
Are closing in to seal your doom.
And though you fight to stay alive,
Your body starts to shiver,
For no mere mortal can resist
The evil of the thriller.

Wanna Be Startin' Somethin'

Words and Music by Michael Jackson

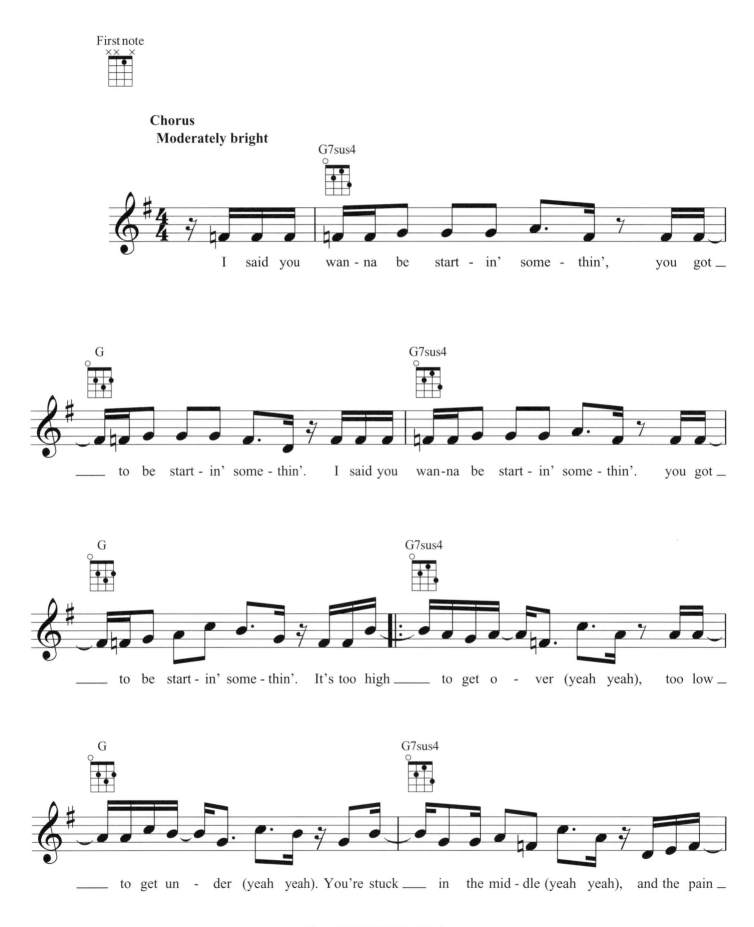

wan-na be start-in' some-thin', you got ___ to be start-in' some-thin'. It's too high ___

___ to get o-ver (yeah, yeah), too low ___ to get un-der (yeah yeah). You're stuck ___

___ in the mid-dle (yeah yeah), and the pain ___ is thun-der (yeah yeah). It's too high ___

___ to get o-ver (yeah yeah), too low ___ to get un-der (yeah yeah). You're stuck ___

1.

To Coda

___ in the mid-dle (yeah yeah), and the pain ___ is thun-der (yeah yeah). 2. You love ___

2., 3.

Bridge

___ is thun-der (yeah yeah). You're a veg-'ta-ble, ___ you're a

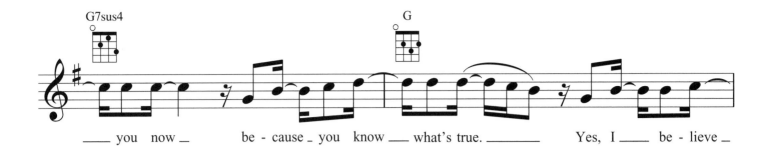

_____ you now ___ be - cause _ you know ___ what's true. _____ Yes, I _____ be - lieve _

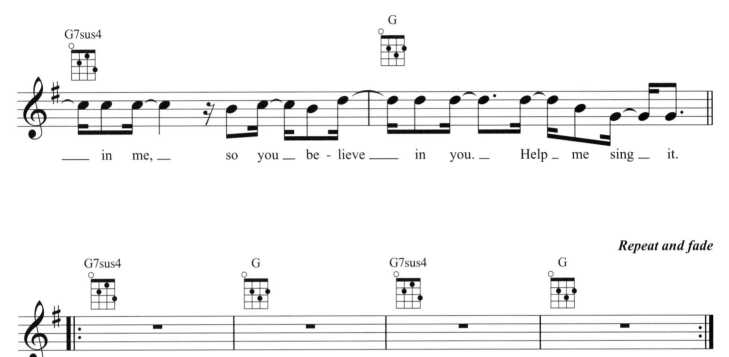

_____ in me, ___ so you __ be - lieve _____ in you. ___ Help _ me sing ___ it.

Repeat and fade

Vocal ad lib.

Additional Lyrics

2. You love to pretend that you're good
   When you're always up to no good.
   You really can't make him hate her,
   So your tongue became a razor.
   Someone's always tryin'
   To keep my baby cryin'.
   Treacherous, cunnin', declinin',
   You got my baby cryin'.

3. Billie Jean is always talkin'
   When nobody else is talkin',
   Tellin' lies and rubbin' shoulders,
   So they could call her mouth a motor.
   Someone's always tryin'
   To start my baby cryin'.
   Talkin', squealin', spyin',
   Sayin' you just wanna be startin' somethin'.

4. If you can't feed your baby,
   Then don't have a baby.
   And don't think maybe,
   If you can't feed your baby.
   You'll be always tryin'
   To stop that child from cryin'.
   Hustlin', stealin', lyin',
   Now baby's slowly dyin'.

Will You Be There

Written by Michael Jackson

You Are Not Alone

Words and Music by Robert Kelly

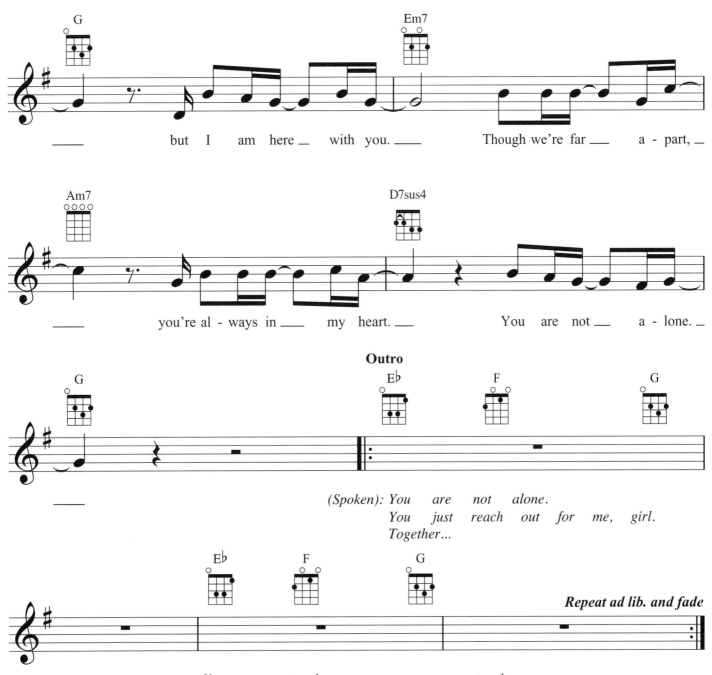

but I am here ___ with you. ___ Though we're far ___ a - part, ___

you're al - ways in ___ my heart. ___ You are not ___ a - lone. ___

Outro

___

(Spoken): You are not alone.
You just reach out for me, girl.
Together...

Repeat ad lib. and fade

You are not alone,   *not alone.*
In the morning in the evening, not alone... not alone...   *you and me, not alone...*

Additional Lyrics

2., 4. You are not alone.
I am here with you.
Though you're far away,
I am here to stay.
You are not alone.
I am here with you.
Though we're far apart,
You're always in my heart.
But you are not alone.

3. Just the other night
I thought I heard you cry,
Asking me to go
And hold you in my arms.
I can hear your breaths,
Your burdens I will bear.
But first I need you here,
Then forever can begin.

You Rock My World

Words and Music by Fred Jerkins III, Lashawn Ameen Daniels, Michael Jackson, Rodney Jerkins and Nora Payne

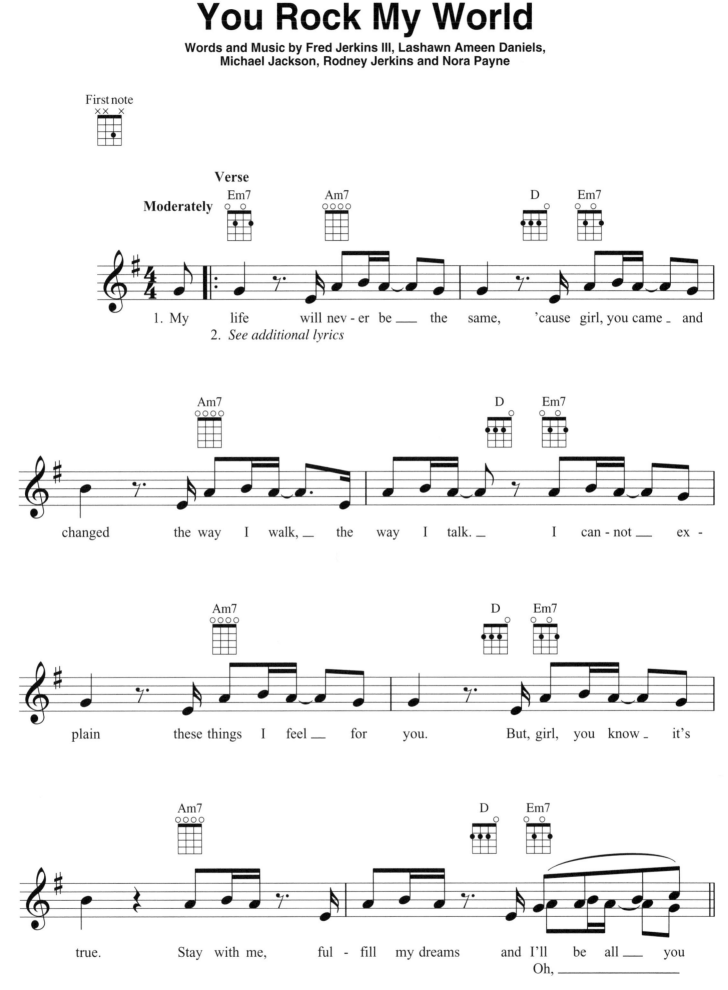

Cmaj7   Am7   D6   Em7   Bm7

I'll nev - er get __ e - nough, that's-a why __

C7sus4   D7sus4

D.S. al Coda

__ I al - ways have __ to have __ you here.

⊕ Coda   Am7   N.C.

The rar - est love, who'd think I'd find some-one __ like you __ to call mine?

Additional Lyrics

2. In time, I knew that love would bring such happiness to me.
   I tried to keep my sanity, I've waited patiently.
   Girl, you know it seems my life is so complete.
   A love that's true because of you.
   Keep doing what you do. Oh, ooh.

Pre-Chorus: Think that I've finally found the perfect love
   I've searched for all my life.
   Oh, who'd think I'd find such a perfect love
   That's awesomely so right? (Oh, girl.)

The Way You Make Me Feel

Words and Music by Michael Jackson

I'll pick you up in my car and we'll paint __ the town.
Just prom - ise, ba - by, you'll love me for - ev - er - more.

Just kiss me, ba - by, and tell me __ twice __
I swear I'm keep - in' you sat - is - fied, __

that you're the one for me. } The way you make me feel. __
'cause you're the one for me. }

Chorus

__ (The way you make me feel.) You real - ly turn me on. __

__ (You real - ly turn me on.) You knock me off of my feet. __

__ (You knock me off of my feet.) My lone - ly days are gone. __

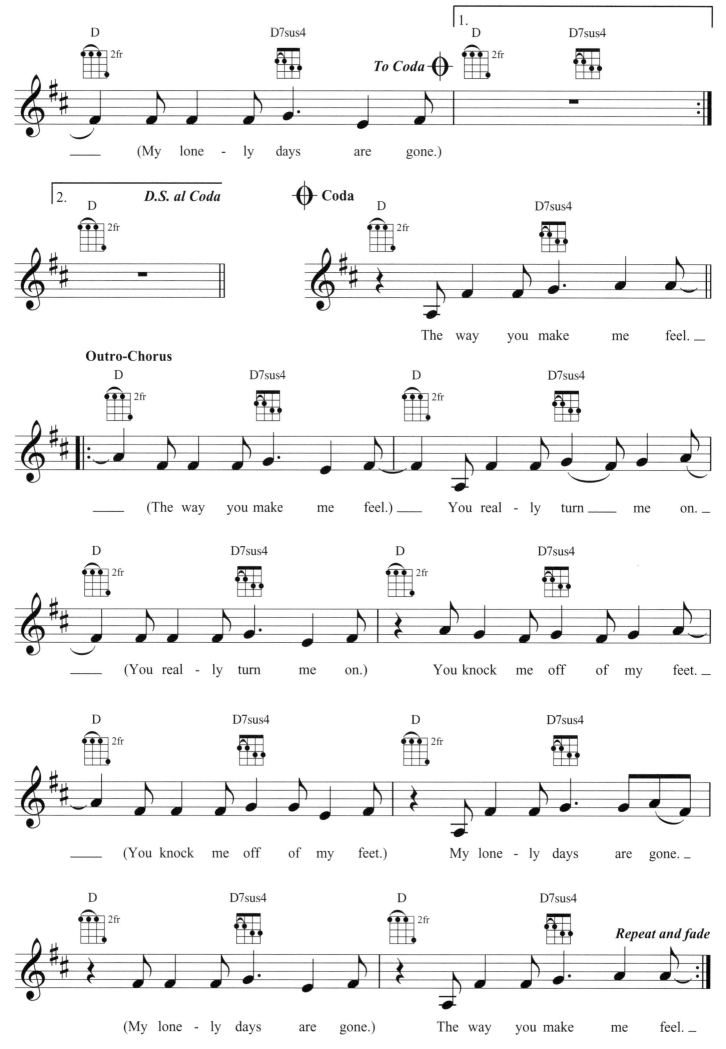